MOODS OF THE
YORKSHIRE COAST

IAN CARSTAIRS

HALSGROVE

First published in Great Britain in 2005

Title page: *Ammonite fossil*

British Library Cataloguing-in-Publication Data
A CIP record for this title is available from the British Library

ISBN 1 84114 446 0

HALSGROVE
Halsgrove House
Lower Moor Way
Tiverton, Devon EX16 6SS
T: 01884 243242
F: 01884 243325

sales@halsgrove.com
www.halsgrove.com

Printed and bound by D'Auria Industrie Grafiche Spa, Italy

Thanks are due to my good friend Patrick Ferguson who accompanied me on many excursions to the coast and who shared the frustration that the weather would be mostly either like the Mediterranean or plain flat grey and raining, neither of which conditions are particularly conducive to portraying a variety and extremes of moods; and to Jan Knowlson and my parents Teresa and Archer Carstairs for their inexhaustible help and support with my projects.

Introduction

If Yorkshire is 'God's own country' – as it is often described – then this therefore must surely be 'God's own coast'. And what a dramatic and extraordinary place it is. From the highest cliffs in eastern England at Boulby Head near Staithes, to the extraordinary Spurn Peninsula, hanging like Yorkshire's tail into the mouth of the Humber, it is a place of natural extremes.

But here too in Scarborough we find an original Victorian seaside town, with its sisters, Bridlington, Filey, Whitby, Saltburn and Redcar, to either side. With the coming of the railways, in the latter part of the nineteenth and first half of the twentieth centuries, these were the great destinations to relax and enjoy yourself for the burgeoning populations of the urban and industrial centres of Middlesbrough, Hull and the West Riding. And today they still remain hugely popular, especially for day-visits.

Like all coasts, the Yorkshire coast is not static; it is ever-changing, with the sea eroding a bit here or adding a bit there. And political boundaries which bring with them name changes have come and gone, and then changed again. This made me think: how exactly should I define where the coast of Yorkshire begins and ends? Of all the modern 'Regions' of England, this is the only one to include its own name. Yorkshire is indeed like a 'country', and since the coast is where the land ends, I have exercised a little license in my definition of where it lies.

I decided to start it at the Tees Transporter Bridge in Middlesbrough, until 1974 in the old North Riding of Yorkshire, and end it at the Humber Bridge, where the coast once lay before the last Ice Age. So, the bridges, the first roads inland into Yorkshire from north and south are my 'fullstops', and the coast's limits are defined by two memorable structures – one a fascinating solution to crossing a river and the other the most elegant feat of engineering I know. And if I needed another excuse to include them, I can also rely on the fact that in navigation law, tidal waters are considered to be arms of the sea – and the tide reaches beyond both of these places.

This is therefore an introduction to *my* Yorkshire coast, and I hope the selection of photographs will encourage you to explore and enjoy it throughout the year, as the seasons, the wind, the light and the moods you will experience change; sometimes subtly, and at other times with dramatic effect.

Ian Carstairs
2005

LOCATION MAP

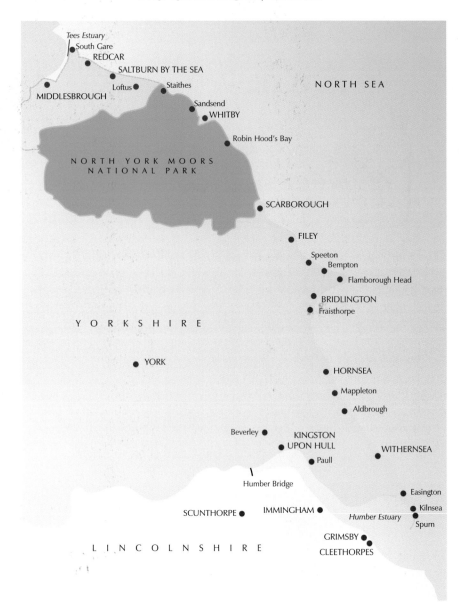

Tees Estuary
South Gare
REDCAR
SALTBURN BY THE SEA
NORTH SEA
Loftus • Staithes
MIDDLESBROUGH
Sandsend
WHITBY

Robin Hood's Bay

NORTH YORK MOORS
NATIONAL PARK

SCARBOROUGH

• FILEY

Speeton
Bempton
Flamborough Head

BRIDLINGTON
Fraisthorpe

Y O R K S H I R E

• YORK

• HORNSEA

Mappleton

Aldbrough

Beverley •
KINGSTON
UPON HULL
WITHERNSEA
Paull

Humber Bridge

Easington

SCUNTHORPE •
IMMINGHAM •
Kilnsea
Humber Estuary
Spurn

GRIMSBY
CLEETHORPES

L I N C O L N S H I R E

Low light over the Tees Estuary
Rising on Cross Fell in the North Pennines, 80 miles (130 kms) away, the
River Tees drains into the North Sea between Hartlepool and Redcar.

Tees Transporter Bridge
Opened in 1911, this is the largest working bridge of its kind in the world,
linking Middlesbrough with the road to Hartlepool. People and vehicles are
winched across the River Tees in a 'gondola' – a mobile section of road –
suspended from overhead cables. It takes ninety seconds.

A sense of isolation
The 360-degree vista from South Gare, a breakwater constructed in the nineteenth century to shelter the mouth of the Tees, reveals an extraordinary variety
in its surroundings, as shown on pages 8 to 13.

Rapid expansion
In 1801 the total population of Middlesbrough was just over 1000; by 1901 it
had reached almost 100,000, and a century later, 135,000 as industries based
on coal, iron, chemicals and later steel developed along the Tees Estuary.

The power of the sun captured on earth
Hartlepool nuclear power station, seen across the Tees Estuary.

Unity of purpose
The South Gare Fishermen's Association huts, huddled together behind
the dunes, display a definite sense of common purpose.

Paddy's Hole
Reputedly named after the Irish labourers who built South Gare, this delight-
ful harbour contrasts markedly with the heavy industry and shipping nearby.
Mercifully there are no souvenir shops, no advertising and no visitor centre;
Paddy's Hole and South Gare are good for the soul.

Coatham Sands
South Gare and the Tees Estuary are part of an internationally-important
wildlife site for birds – which happily co-exist alongside major industry.

Sands and steelworks
Evening light dramatises the backdrop of heavy industry near Redcar.

Sole survivor
Completed in 1869, Saltburn's
Victorian iron pier is the only one left
in the north east. It can be accessed on
foot or by the cliff lift.

Previous: **The value of space**
Outside Teesmouth, the open sea has
been eyed-up for a potential multi-
tower complex of wind turbines, which
if it ever was built, would rob the local
coast of its expansive sense of freedom.

Coastal cliffs
Just east of Saltburn, we get a clear hint of the precipitous character of the
coast for the next 35 miles (60 kms), much of it, between Staithes and
Scarborough, lying within the North York Moors National Park.

Sands…
A fine beach, Cattersty Sands, is tucked secretly round
the headland from Skinningrove.

... and ironstone
From the mid-ninteenth century until the 1960s, East Cleveland was a centre
for iron-stone mining both inland and on the coast. The Tom Leonard Mining
Museum in Skinningrove tells the story of daily life in the mines.

Behind the coast
Behind the East Cleveland coast, as here in Loftus, lies beautiful countryside
with attractive wooded valleys, farmland and grassy areas. The remains of iron
mining spoil heaps stand out like conical volcanoes on the horizon.

Water avens
A pretty plant, found in a few grassy, damp
and shady places inland from the coast.

Into the soul of the Universe
With the deepest working shaft in Europe descending to 3640 feet
(1100m), Britain's only potash mine extends some 4½ miles (7km) out
to sea. It is also the underground home for leading scientific experiments
into the existence of Dark Matter, particles thought to play a large part
in the structure of the Universe.

High point
At 650 feet (200m), Boulby Cliff is the highest coastal cliff in eastern England.

Historic harbour
Nestling in the mouth of Roxby Beck, Staithes was a home to the young James Cook. Taking a line due north, the Shetland Islands are the only land standing between Staithes and the Arctic.

Conservation …
The seemingly haphazard
arrangement of buildings in Staithes
reflect successive generations'
maximum use of limited space.

… and tradition
A modern version of a Staithes
bonnet, historically worn by women
in the village, keeps the style and
tradition alive.

Times past
Staithes was once one of the largest fishing ports in the
north-east. The design of the traditional Yorkshire coble boat
is said to be directly descended from the Viking longship.

A Victorian creation
Port Mulgrave harbour, seen here before the sea took its toll, was built in the 1850s specifically for the shipment of iron ore, extracted both from shafts near the jetty and a tunnel into the cliff, to the blast furnaces of the Tees and Tyne.

Cleveland Way
The 108-mile (173km) Cleveland Way National Trail follows the clifftops
from Saltburn to Filey. Here it passes through Port Mulgrave.

Descent to the coast
With high cliffs, few settlements have developed along this wild stretch
of the coast. A steep road leads down into Runswick Bay.

An exposed position
Evidence exists for settlement here before Roman times, but Runswick Bay has
suffered the effects of serious erosion and landslips over the centuries.

Quarried away
In the late eighteenth century, quarrying and processing of alum shale,
used in the manufacture of fix for the dyeing industry, transformed
the shape of the headland of Kettleness.

Sandsend Ness
Like Kettleness and other areas of this coast, Sandsend Ness
was quarried away two centuries ago for alum shale.

Sandsend
Sunlight shafts onto the breakers. There can be strong and dangerous currents along the beach.

Turning stone into houses
Reflecting the local geology, sandstone was used extensively in the past as a source of building material in the northern part of the North York Moors National Park.

Towards Whitby
A long sandy beach stretches from Sandsend to Whitby, which lies
hidden from view inside the mouth of the River Esk.

An Easter present
The present method for fixing the date of Easter was set at the Synod of Whitby, held in AD663 at St Hilda's Celtic monastery, high on the cliff-top above Whitby.

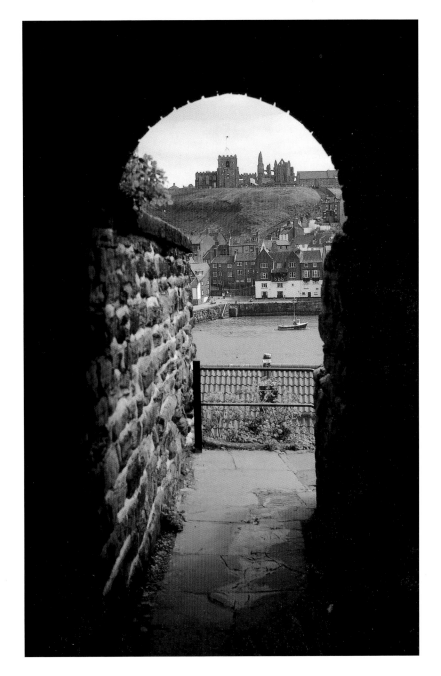

Overleaf: **An unspoilt town**
One of the least modernised and 'undeveloped' towns in the country, Whitby is of international heritage quality. Famed also as the fictional landing place of Bram Stoker's Dracula, who came ashore here as dog, it is very popular with Goths.

Whitby Abbey
Set in a spectacular though seriously exposed position, the Benedictine
house founded here in 1071 near the site of the seventh-century Celtic
monastery, was dissolved by Henry VIII in 1540.

A unique church
St Mary's Church, Whitby, is renowned for its considerable seating capacity. The roof was constructed by ship's carpenters and bears a close resemblance to the deck of a wooden sailing ship.

…and an atmospheric graveyard
With the ruins of the Abbey looming behind, St Mary's graveyard is a moving and slightly mysterious place, especially on foggy days or at night.

199 steps
A long series of steps link Whitby
headland, St Mary's Church and the
Abbey with the town. Easy going down,
rather harder coming up!

An ancient port
The suffix 'by' denotes a Viking origin to the name of Whitby, which was an
important port for them. With a strong sea running, the calming
effect of the harbour breakwaters on the waves is clearly visible.

Safety at sea
Berthed on the east side of the River Esk,
the modern lifeboat is moored permanently
in the harbour when not at sea.

A gift of friendship and a nautical hero

A pair of 17 foot (5.5m) jawbones from a bowhead whale were presented by the people of Anchorage, Alaska, with which Whitby is twinned, to replace an older deteriorating pair erected as a memorial to William Scoresby. Whitby was a major whaling port in the nineteenth century. In the background, a statue commemorates the eighteenth-century explorer Captain James Cook, who sailed from Whitby in the *Endeavour*.

Historic sailing vessels
A one-fifth scale replica of Captain James Cook's HM Bark *Endeavour*, built locally using traditional techniques, is moored in Whitby harbour. In the background is a modern reconstruction of an eighteenth century man-o-war, *Grand Turk*, built in Turkey and completed in 1996.

Grand Turk
The carvings and colours demonstrate the complexity and detail in the design of historic naval vessels. The *Grand Turk* is based on original drawings of a frigate named *Blandford*.

Survivor of the Sixties

Having largely avoided the impact of sixties-town-centre redevelopments, Whitby's streets are still lined with traditional shops and houses *(top right)*. Among these are the Magpie Café *(bottom right)* – a well-known supplier of fish and chips – and the entrance to Grape Lane *(left)*, the location of the beautifully-presented Captian Cook Memorial Museum, based in the house where he served his seaman's apprenticeship.

Precarious properties

The construction of a substantial sea wall in 1975 now protects the lovely fishing village of Robin Hood's Bay from the impact of the sea and storms. In the past, it was a not infrequent occurrence for buildings to slip over the edge.

Along the shore
The rocky pools formed where softer layers of rock are worn away faster than the layers above and below are renowned for their marine life. Robin Hood's Bay is also famous for its fossils.

Turned to stone
The hard parts of an ammonite's body, locked in time some one hundred and eighty million years ago.

Across the bay
Low tide at the September equinox in Robin Hood's Bay reveals the
extent of complex concentric layers of eroded rock created by the sea.

Sudden change
As the land rises, the soil changes from good farmland along the coast to the
poorer soils on the sandstone, where heather grows today.

The vast moor
Inland from the coast, the heather moorland of the North York Moors stretches
for more than 100 square miles (160 sq kms). The natural obstacle of the
moors, with their harsh winter weather and historically poor roads, gave rise in
the past to the saying that 'the only way to Whitby is by the sea'.

Autumn in the air
Looking towards Robin Hood's Bay from Fylingthorpe across the
coastal farmland. 'Thorpe' is another place-name ending which
denotes a Viking settlement.

Left behind by time
The remains of old windmills, from the days before the internal combustion
engine and electrical power, are quite common along the coast.

A commanding view
Harder rocks at sea level have meant that Scarborough Castle Hill
has eroded at a slower pace than the bays lying either side of it.
This wonderful vantage point, seen here over looking North Bay,
has been a strategic location since prehistoric and Roman times.

An original holiday town
Tucked in from Castle Hill are Scarborough town, the sea
front amusements and the main holiday beach.

Perched on a hill
The oldest parts of Scarborough
Castle were constructed between
1135 and 1138 during the reign of
King Stephen. The foundations of a
Roman signal station are found near
the seaward edge of the hill.

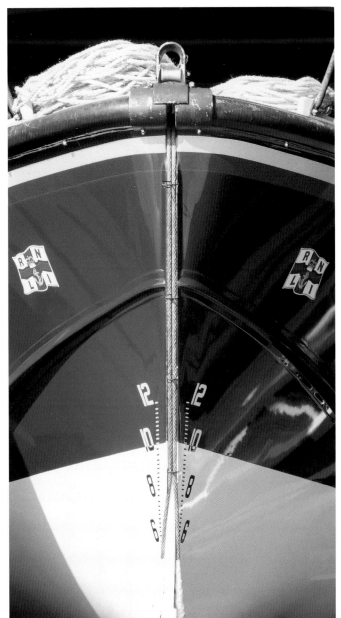

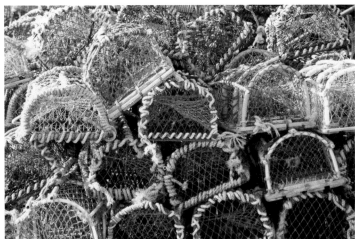

Facets of life
A walk along Scarborough harbour reveals many sides of the
character of this archetypal seaside town – lobster pots,
a fun-fair wheel and the lifeboat in its station – all just
a short distance away from each other.

Home from the sea
Looking south from Scarborough Castle Hill reveals a wide
vista across the harbour and town.

Who cares?
Some obviously do! On-going maintenance on the quayside.

St Mary's Church, Scarborough
Standing in an imposing position above the town, St Mary's is the last resting place of Anne Brontë, the only one of the Brontë sisters not to be buried in Haworth, where the talented literary family lived.

A 'museum of a museum'
An internationally-
important museum,
The Rotunda was especially
constructed in 1829 to house
the collections of William
Smith, the father of modern
geology, and is now a
museum piece itself.

Stormy weather on the way
Marine Drive, running round the seaward side of Castle Hill between
North and South Bays, is an exhilarating walk, but experiences the
full effect of stormy seas and heavy weather.

High summer in the harbour
All the main harbours along the Yorkshire coast are
popular for recreational use.

Trail's end
The Cleveland Way National Trail arches round the North York
Moors National Park from Helmsley to Filey Brigg. From here the
79-mile (127km) Wolds Way, another National Trail, winds its way
through the Yorkshire Wolds to the Humber Bridge.

A sheltering finger
Like other headlands along the coast, Filey Brigg gives
shelter to the town and with its long views, it is
a popular place for visitors to the area.

Rocks and rockpools
Low tide reveals the abundance of the marine
environment surrounding Filey Brigg.

A good place for the birds
Filey Brigg is an excellent location for birdwatching, particularly at
migration time. It is not unusual in winter to see dozens of oystercatchers
and redshank feeding in the grass on the car park, when the tide
forces them up off the rocks and beach.

Made by the ice
Virtually the whole of the Yorkshire coast is covered with a cap of boulder clay,
carried here as ground-up material from the land over which the ice passed
during the last Ice Age and deposited as the ice retreated.

A world between land and sea
The Brigg is well-used by
fishermen and also by birds
such as the shag *(below)* which
can occasionally be seen on
the rocks at the tip when
the tide is out.

Overleaf: **Looming cliffs**
Bempton's sheer chalk cliffs,
formed from the bodies of
myriads of sea creatures during
the Cretaceous period between
140 and 65 million years ago,
line the grey horizon on a
late winter's day.

A little gem

Small churches are a feature and havens of quiet throughout the length of the Yorkshire coast. With its massive walls for such a small structure, St Leonard's, Speeton was built before 1100 AD. Like elsewhere in Britain, churches are the single most tangible expression of our heritage across the landscape. Other delightful examples are shown elsewhere on our journey south.

Seabird city
Bempton Cliffs, parts of which
are managed by the Royal Society
for the Protection of Birds, are home
to large sea bird colonies from spring
to mid summer, with thousands of birds
packed onto narrow cliff ledges like a
vertical city. Filey Brigg can
be seen in the distance.

Enigmatic sentinel
A shag stands on alert. Loyal to the coast all year round,
these enigmatic birds nest near the foot of the cliffs.

On the edge of a ledge
Higher up the cliffs, the narrow ledges are home to razorbills and guillemots *(below)*, while puffins *(right)* nest in burrows in crevices or in the soil of the cliff-top.

Bird with a crash helmet
Higher still, gannets have their largest mainland colony in Britain.
Our biggest sea bird, it has no external nostrils and a specially thickened
skull, which enable it to dive from height into the water after food.

Caller of the cliffs
Kittiwakes attach their nests of seaweed to the ledges with mud.
Their distinctive 'kit-e-wake' call is perhaps the most evocative sound
of this wild and exposed place.

Atlantic grey seal
Off-shore, marine mammals, such as dolphins and seals, sometimes pass by.

A foggy day …
Winds off the North Sea can
shroud the cliffs in fog, even when
the weather is glorious not far inland.
While you cannot see the birds,
you can still hear them and, more
significantly, smell them as the
wind blows up the cliff face.

... and a sunny day
The chalk cliffs which rise south of
Filey continue on to Flamborough
Head in the distance, before petering
out just north of Bridlington.

The Dotterel and the White Horse

How come a local pub near Speeton is named the Dotterel, after this rare bird which nests high in the mountains of Scotland? The suggestion is that these birds used to stop-off in this area on their spring migration north.

The extraordinary glazed tiles make the White Horse, Bempton, a memorable building, though one suspects they would be extremely difficult to replace when damaged.

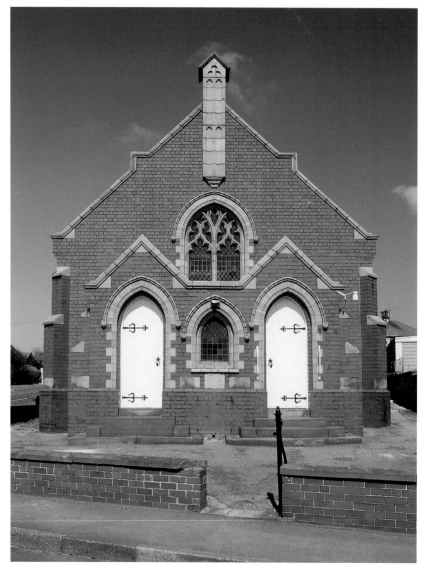

Edwardian chapel
The strong design and coloured brick make for an imposing building in the
Bempton streetscene. Initials carved into blocks along the side are those of
people who donated money towards its construction. It was completed in 1903.

The Old Lighthouse
Standing in an area of Flamborough known as Little Denmark, named after the king of Denmark who reputedly once laid claim to it, this chalk-built structure was completed in 1674. And yes, it does lean.

The 'New' Lighthouse
Constructed without the use of
scaffolding in 1806, Flamborough's
'new' lighthouse is working and fully
automated – and open to visitors.

Lost in the mist of time
No-one is certain of the date of Flamborough Castle, which is also known as
Constable Castle, though some think it to be no earlier than the reign of
Edward III. Constructed from chalk, it is now in ruins.

Chalk readily at hand
Chalk provided a ready supply of local material for
many old buildings in the area.

Before the special relationship
On September 23, 1779, United States ships under the command of John Paul Jones engaged
ships of the Royal Navy in the Battle of Flamborough Head. Jones won the battle, taking
many prisoners. The dramatic cliffs and coastal waters are today important sites for wildlife.

Signs of spring
The arrival of spring on the headland is marked by cheerful groups of
primroses dotted across the grassy slopes.

Rock shaped by water
Flamborough Head has a fine example of a wave-cut platform in
addition to other dramatic coastal landforms.

An open text book
The sheltered cove, accessible down a steep track and steps, is a popular
location for educational visits to study geology and natural history.

The cutting edge
Softer layers at the foot of the cliff are being cut back by the sea. In time, the cliff above will collapse and the erosion will move on.

Nature the artist
Stones washed from the cliff or dropped when the ice retreated and rounded by
the sea make an attractive study in greys and whites.

The working coast
From Bridlington harbour wall, views of the fishing quay bring home the realities of making a living from the sea.

Waiting for the holiday-makers
The name Bridlington is rooted in times before the Vikings arrived –
the ending, 'ton' denoting Anglian origins. At Bridlington the chalk cliffs
cease and from here all the way south to Spurn Point, some 35 miles (56 kms),
the coastline is formed from low boulder clay cliffs.

A disappearing coastline
Holderness, the large area of land forming a triangle south from Bridlington to
Spurn Point and Hull, is all soft clay. Where cliffs limited the settlements to
the north, here the rate of erosion – one of the fastest in the world – means
that there are even fewer towns and villages.

Traps on the beach
The lowest-lying areas between the Tees and the Humber at Fraisthorpe raised
the fear of sea-borne invasion here during the Second World War. Concrete
defences were lined along the beach to impede such an attack.

Loss of support
Through time, the sea has 'rearranged' the old defences, removing
the support from this concrete pill box.

The sea creeps on
A little more of Yorkshire slides into the sea in this close-up of another landslip in the boulder clay. Conscious of the ever-advancing waves, Fraisthorpe villagers marked the end of the second millennium witha tablet recording the distance from the sea on 1 January, 2000.

ON 1.1.2000 A.D.
THIS MILLENNIUM STONE
WAS 1650 METRES
(1800 YARDS)
FROM THE SEA.

An evolving building
There is something pleasant about this building which has been repaired
with different materials suited to the needs of the moment, and not
modernised wholesale. It uses cobbles from the beach, old bricks, new
bricks and corrugated asbestos for the roof.

Winter on the beach – Hornsea
Running seas and sullen skies merge into the grey horizon, punctuated by
the distant spire of All Saints' Church, Mappleton, on a freezing winter day.
The groynes (barriers on the beach) were constructed to try to halt the
sands from being washed away to the south.

Ice Age dusk
A relict of the Ice Age, Hornsea Mere is the largest
freshwater lake in east Yorkshire.

Mute swan
Hornsea Mere is managed as a nature reserve by the Royal Society for the
Protection of Birds, and stately mute swans are among the beneficiaries.

Yellow flag or iris
A plant of the water's edge and wet and boggy
places, and the orginal for the fleur-de-lis.

Built from the beach
Continuing the theme of local
buildings reflecting the surrounding geology,
All Saints' Church, Mappleton is
constructed from cobbles.

More cobbles
With its distinctive square tower, the fourteenth century St Bartholomew's Church in Aldbrough is another fine example of a building constructed using cobbles. An ancient pre-Norman sundial is located on a nave wall.

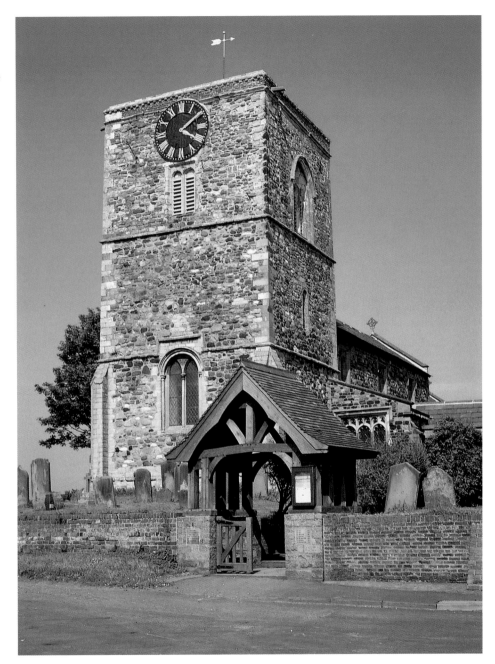

A view of erosion – in summer ...
Bathed in sunshine, it is difficult to imagine that the Holderness coast
experiences a continuous attack from the sea.

... and on a late winter's day
A brown tinge to the crests of the waves is clear evidence that the
water is loaded with silt eroded from the coast, which the sea is transporting
southwards by a process known as long-shore drift.

Keeping up ap-pier-ances
All that remains of Withernsea's 1200 foot (370m) long pier which collapsed
in a storm in 1880, having previously been hit by several ships. The final 15
feet (5m) was demolished in the early twentieth century. A long seat on the
pavement, made in the shape of the pier, bears witness to the pier of the past.

Holding the line
Huge boulders have been laid along the top of the
beach at Withernsea to lessen the impact of the waves.

SISTER KIRKES

LEGEND
TELLS OF TWO SISTERS
BUILDING SEPARATE CHURCHES
AFTER ARGUING OVER THE STYLE
OF A JOINTLY FUNDED CHURCH.
ONE WANTED A SPIRE THE OTHER A TOWER.
THESE TWO BUILDINGS BECAME KNOWN
AS THE SISTERKIRKES.

THE SEA EVENTUALLY CLAIMED BOTH
OF THE CHURCHES, ERODING THE CHURCH OF
ST. MARY THE VIRGIN WITHERNSEA AROUND 1444,
& ST. PETER'S CHURCH OWTHORNE BETWEEN 1786 AND 1824.

STONES FROM THE CHURCHES WERE
REUSED IN THE BUILDING OF
ST. NICHOLAS CHURCH WITHERNSEA AND
ST. MARY THE VIRGIN RIMSWELL.

HUMAN REMAINS FOUND ON
THE BEACH FROM ST PETER'S
WERE REINTERRED AT
RIMSWELL.

Long-gone churches
An inscribed stone emphasises the course of history in an area
which is so vulnerable to the sea.

Lighthouse at the end of the street
Unlike other lighthouses along the Yorkshire coast, Withernsea's is
in the middle of the town. Now redundant, it houses a small
museum and is open to the public.

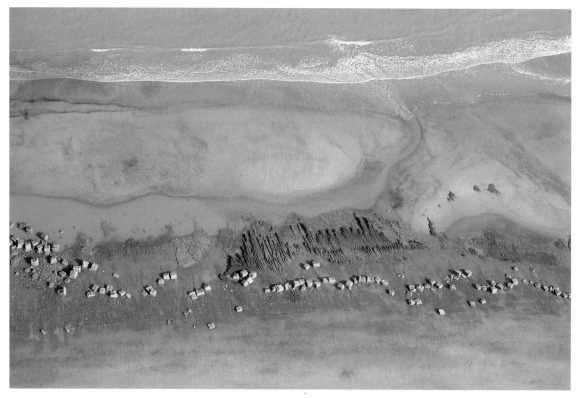

Defences lie defenceless
In this vertical aerial view near Kilnsea, concrete defences lie strewn along the beach like a set of discarded children's building blocks. Outcrops of peat from prehistoric times *(centre)* are being exposed by the waves.

A moving story

At 3 miles (5 kms) long and in places barely 55 yards (50m) wide, the Spurn peninsula is one of the most unusual places in England. Formed from material eroded from the Holderness coast, left to its own devices it would constantly creep westwards. Today it is owned and managed as a nature reserve by the Yorkshire Wildlife Trust.

High and Low Lights

The now-redundant Spurn lighthouse, a listed historical building, was built in 1895 to replace an earlier lighthouse built by John Smeaton in 1776, which once stood next to it. In the foreground is the remains of a companion Low Light to Smeaton's lighthouse, used subsequently as an explosives store and later as a water storage tower, hence the tank on the top.

Life at the point
On a misty day from the top of the lighthouse, the remoteness of the
peninsula is palpable in a world where you know you are joined to the land,
but feel as though you are in the middle of the sea. The houses on the point are
the homes of the Spurn lifeboat crew, the only full-time crew in the country.
The Humber pilots are also based here.

A hopeless task
In Victorian times, defences were constructed to try to halt the erosion,
but they simply stored up trouble by stopping the peninsula moving while
the land north of the root continued to erode westwards. In this photograph
taken in 1981, in front of the lighthouse is the circular old lighthouse
compound, where the lighthouse keepers and their families lived.

The power of time and tide

In this vertical view taken in 1981 *(top left)*, the sea is knocking on the
door of the circular old lighthouse compound, in the centre of which
once stood Smeaton's 1776 lighthouse. By 1990 *(bottom left)*, the sea had
long broken through, and today you can barely spot a trace – just part
of a concrete rim shows among the vegetation.

Whale ribs
Remains of old defences, beaten by the sea, protrude like the ribs
of a massive whale exposed on the beach.

Overleaf: **A hub of activity**
Smeaton's Low Light with lifeboat
and Humber pilots' jetty inside the
mouth of the Humber.

Watching and fishing
The peninsula is internationally renowned for the study of bird migration.
In autumn, tens of thousands of birds are funnelled down the narrow strip as
they bid to stay over land as long as possible, before the short journey
across to the Lincolnshire coast. It is also a good place to see passing
ships and for fishing.

Ship's guide
A pilot cutter departs to meet and guide a ship off the Humber Estuary.

Glorious mud

The vast mudflats of Spurn Bight, seen from
Kilnsea, provide extensive feeding grounds
for wading birds and wildfowl. The shores
and mudflats of Spurn and the Humber
Estuary are specially protected by
European legislation for their wildlife,
such as the ringed plover *(right)*.

Power in the wind
A farm-based wind power station
close to Easington.

An island of calm
Standing far outside Paull village, the churchyard of this beautiful isolated
building is carpeted with primroses in spring. Next door behind the trees is
an unusual military museum set in an old Napoleonic-era fort overlooking
the Humber. One of its extraordinary exhibits shown
overleaf can be spotted over the fort wall.

The last giant
Dominating the exhibits inside Paull Fort is the last remaining example in the
world of a huge Blackburn Beverley troop transport aircraft.

On the waterfront
The spectacular view across the wide estuary from Paull Fort
emphasises the strategic significance of the location. On the horizon
lie the South Killingholm oil refineries and the port of Immingham
in North Lincolnshire, 6 miles (10 kms) away.

A mini-lighthouse
Built by Trinity House in 1836, this diminutive lighthouse
and its associated buildings is an aesthetically-satisfying group.
Set on a bend in the Humber Estuary, it enjoys a clear view
to the Humber Bridge, 10 miles (16kms) away.

Passing traffic
A fuel barge works its way downstream, with the colossal span of
the Humber Bridge lining the distant horizon.

Journey's end
Old barges double as a security barrier to protect a small boat yard.

Salt End
BP's Salt End chemical works is
supplied directly from a jetty
protruding out into the Humber.

River Hull
The origins of the name of Kingston-upon-Hull recall when the manor
on the River Hull was bought by Edward I in 1293. The village was
originally known as Wyke, meaning a creek. The barrier in the distance
is closed to protect the modern city in times of flood surge.

King Bill
This gold-leafed statue of King William III faces up Low Gate by the remarkable Victorian underground toilets nearby. Some say if the Trinity Church clock strikes 13, he gets off his horse to pay a visit!

Overleaf: **The Deep**
Hull's fabulous submarium, 'The Deep', is housed in a striking building on the water-front at the mouth of the River Hull. Beyond, the port of Hull is one of the premier ports in the United Kingdom.

Civic pride
The magnificent Hull Guildhall rivals anything that Whitehall can offer.
It is topped by two dramatic roof sculptures: 'Maritime Prowess' seen
at the far end of the building shows Aphrodite in a boat drawn by horses
rising from the waves, and 'Strength' out of picture at the near end
shows Britannia riding a chariot flanked by lions.

A proud legacy
The Museum Quarter of Hull exudes an air of calm, seen
reflected in this view of the gardens.

A glorious past
A museum exhibit moored in the River Hull, the *Arctic Corsair* is a reminder
of Hull's once extensive fishing fleet, now reduced to a few vessels.

An icon for freedom

A museum based in William Wilberforce's house is a focus for one of the most significant characters in British history who, as MP for Hull, steered through the abolition of slavery throughout the British Empire. Behind the house, the quiet of a small formal garden *(below)* is a place to contemplate the enormity of Wilberforce's achievement.

A great parish church
Reflected in the windows behind the Magistrates' Court, Holy Trinity Church
is said to cover the largest area of any parish church in England.

Hull-o?
In the days of nationalised industries, Hull was alone in this country in
having its own telephone system. Its distinctive white phone boxes,
as opposed to red elsewhere, remain a feature of the area.

Old Pilot Office
Now redeveloped, the old Pilot Office
stands on the edge of a delightful
square, near to the embarkation
point for ferries across the Humber
from Hull to New Holland, in the
days before the Humber Bridge
was completed in 1981.

A bridge afar
The gravity-defying span of the Humber Bridge is nowhere better
appreciated than from the end of the old docks, close now to the
retail shopping parks to the west of Hull.

Where engineering meets art
When it opened in 1981, the Humber Bridge was the longest single-span
suspension bridge in the world, with almost a mile (1.5 kms) between its
towers. This is the view from near Barton Clay Pits, outside Yorkshire,
where you are now officially on the Lincolnshire coast.